Lessons From The Rocking Chair

Timeless Stories for Teaching Character

Deb Austin Brown

Lessons From The Rocking Chair
Timeless Stories for Teaching Character
Deb Austin Brown

Produced and published by
CHARACTER DEVELOPMENT GROUP

LESSONS FROM THE ROCKING CHAIR
Timeless Stories for Teaching Character

(919) 967-2110, (919) 967-2139 fax

ISBN 0-9653163-3-5

Fourth Printing 2002

 Printed on Recycled Paper

Contents

Endorsements
Lessons From The Rocking Chair

"Truly excellent stories from a respected teacher!"
Gaston Caperton
Fellow, Harvard University's John F. Kennedy School of Government
Governor, West Virginia 1989-1997

"What a nice collection of *Lessons* for <u>everyone</u>! This work will be a huge inspiration to many."
Steve Wariner
Award Winning Musician / Singer / Songwriter
(Steve has won a CMA Award, 7 BMI Songwriting Awards, and a Grammy! He has had twelve Number-One Hits and twenty-eight Top-Ten Hits on his 16 albums! He was recently inducted as the 72nd member of The Grand Ole Opry.)

"Captivating stories that speak to your heart and bring a smile to your face. You'll want to keep a copy of this book handy at work and home!"
Dr. William Mitchell, author
Winning in the Land of Giants

"Reading *Lessons From The Rocking Chair* will make you feel good inside. It will remind you of the ageless words of wisdom your grandparents taught through the use of stories and parables. It is a book to leave out on the coffee table for all to read... and reread... and reread!"
Michael A. Mitchell
Executive Director
Power of Positive Students International Foundation

"Timeless wisdom, profoundly simple, aimed straight at our hearts. This gem of a book will rock you out of your rut and awaken the best within you."
Dr. Denis Waitley, author
Seeds of Greatness

"Maw Great and Æsop! What a dynamic duo for teaching children the lessons of life... the lessons from the rocking chair!"
Joe Pinner,
Peabody Award Winner
Radio and Television Performer WIS-TV: Columbia, South Carolina

"These old-fashioned stories of encouragement tap into the deep recesses of one's soul....These stories... warm our hearts with all the tenderness of a good love story and remind you what it means to be human. As Nathaniel Branden reminds us: *Telling stories is one of the most powerful ways to teach values and open doors to new possibilities.*"
Mary Ann Weatherman, editor

Author's Note

I hope that a hundred years
after I am dead and forgotten,
men who never heard of me
will be moving to the measure
of these thoughts.

I have found power, magic,
excitement, and promise
in these rocking chair lessons
from the past!
It is my hope that this collection
of rocking chair wisdom
will enrich **your** life
... in wonderful ways!

Acknowledgments

To my great grandmother, Maw Great... Margarette French McKibben Rubenacker: This book is a compilation of the rocking chair lessons you taught me with patience and with love. Because of their wisdom, these lessons have greatly enriched my life! And now, they will enrich the lives of others.

To my parents... Margaret and Jack Austin: Your lessons on family and character built the strong foundation for my life and happiness. I love you both very much!

To my grandmothers... Eugenia Grobmeier McKibben and Nina Webb Austin: You taught me that I was special and capable of anything in life! Your belief in me transcended all of my self-doubts and charted my destiny in powerful ways!

To my sisters and brothers... Ellen, Stephanie, Tom, and Pat: Growing up with you made me very happy! I cherish our heritage and our friendship! Your big sister was always at the desk using up all of the paper in the Austin household. Now you know why!

To my nephews... Brian, Elliott, and Ethan: Being your *Aunt Deb* has made my life happy... and fun! These rocking chair lessons were taught before your time, but their wisdom is ageless. This rich and wonderful heritage is yours for the taking!

To my friend and partner in work... Pat Cline: You've read each word I've written for the last eight years, and loved me through every page! Your feedback and encouragement have brought me to this time and place. This book was written because of your belief in me!

To my hometown friends... Carol Mottesheard, Kathryn Ross, Mike Sidebottom, Jim Vickers, Ronnie Holstein, David Covert, Tom Harmon, Nancy Terlizzi, Doc Brown, Linda Taylor, Chris Ketterly, Jane Roberts, and Doak Turner: Your friendship has made my life happy and rewarding! Old friends are always the *best* friends!

To the great teachers in my life... Lucy Marra at St. Francis School: You taught me everything I know about the English language and turned me on to the power of words! To Professor Brewster at West Virginia University, my first writing instructor: You took a young nineteen year-old girl and taught her that she could make people *feel* things with her writing! Your teachings will live on in these pages.

To my friends and colleagues at The Power of Positive Students International Foundation, The Institute for Family Success, and Youcan University for Kids in Myrtle Beach, South Carolina... Dr. William Mitchell, Carolyn Mitchell, Mike Mitchell, Janey Mitchell, Bill Mitchell, Dr. Gardner McCollum, and Carolyn Davis: You've taught me so much by the example of your lives. Thanks for letting me share in your wisdom *and* your life's work!

To my friends and professional family... The Milken Family Foundation, in Los Angeles, California: Your belief that teaching is *the* most important profession has given me wings! Thanks for your respect and generosity!

To the teachers, parents, and students in my hometown... St. Albans, West Virginia and my school district... Kanawha County Schools: Working together has taught me that teamwork, in any community, is always the *best* work!

To the professionals at Character Development Group who helped with the editing, layout, design, and marketing of this book... Mary Ann Weatherman, Paul Turley, Dixon J. Smith, and Phil Vincent: With your magic wand of patience and talent, you've transformed me from a writer into an author! You have my unconditional respect and gratitude!

To a wonderful artist and friend... Karen Kersey: Your insight and talent in creating the cover have made this book even more special! Thanks for working so closely with me to create a cover that helps me *feel* Maw Great's presence in this book!

To the talented men who generously gave endorsements for this book... Michael Mitchell, Dr. William Mitchell, Dr. Denis Waitley, Joe Pinner, Steve Wariner, and Governor Gaston Caperton: You've proven Mark Twain right: "... the really great make you feel that you, too, can become great!" You are men of success, but more importantly... you are men of *value*!

To my new friend and colleague... Dr. Philip Vincent: You took a chance on a small-town girl with a big-time dream. Thanks for reading this book and believing in its value! Because of *you*, my publishing dream has been realized!

To my sons... Aaron and Ben: My love for you is deep, unconditional... and all-encompassing! Being your mom has been the *best* part of my life! Always remember the powerful lessons in this book! From the rocking chair of the past, I pass them on.

Meet... Maw Great!

Maw Great
Margarette French McKibben Rubenacker
1881–1967

Maw Great's Home
Germantown, Kentucky
(Built sometime before the Civil War. Now on *The Historic Register*)

Foreword

When I was a child, my brother and I along with other children in the community would spend many summer evenings listening to our families and neighbors discuss current events and ideas. The range of discussions included politics, social concerns, and proper behaviors and habits for children. Some of the discussions about good behavior were specifically aimed at the children present, myself included, who may have been recently caught engaging in mischief around the neighborhood.

These neighbors and family members were never harsh in their lessons or morals they shared with us. They knew we were children and that we would make mistakes. However they wanted us to avoid repeating them. Some neighbors would always tell us Bible stories to make a point. Others would use old fables or just make–up stories. The lessons and stories were generally enjoyable and always had a moral message. I was fortunate to grow up hearing these stories. I only wish I could remember more of them to share with my daughter.

Lucky for us there are those who seem to remember and can recall a lot of the great moral lessons taught in their youth. Deb Brown is one such person. Deb is a wonderful storyteller who talks to the heart as well as the mind. She can have you laughing at one moment and in serious contemplation at another. She sends us back to another time yet provides a relevant message for the children and adults of today.

Lessons From The Rocking Chair proclaims the wisdom of the generations. Read it and share it with a friend. Perhaps this friend will share it with another. I can think of no greater gift for our children and our society. We know what to do. We know what the good is. The question is whether we are willing to do so. This book will definitely help.

Dr. Philip Fitch Vincent

Introduction

"ONCE UPON A TIME..." is a familiar beginning for the stories of my youth. Each story always ended with, **"And, the moral of the story is..."** During my childhood, stories were told to teach me a lesson. My great grandmother, Maw Great, gave me a rich heritage of *rocking chair wisdom* by the stories told from her chair!

Maw Great lived in a beautiful farmhouse in Kentucky. The farmland was rich and green with promise. Much of my childhood was spent making the trip from the majestic mountain country of West Virginia to visit her. With each visit, I heard more and more stories... and gathered more and more wisdom under my childhood belt.

My great grandmother transmitted family morals and values to me with the stories told from that chair. From the edge of a featherbed, from the front porch swing... and from the rocking chair, I learned the wisdom of the generations that came before me.

Storytellers throughout history have charted social values and direction with the telling of their tales. Long before stories were ever written down, stories were told at family meals, at bedtime, and at town gatherings. Children, through-out the ages, have grown up on stories; adults have clung to their powerful life-lessons. Stories have, therefore, become historical accounts of the moral life and values of each time and culture.

Maw Great used stories to teach me valuable life-lessons. Her favorites were fairy tales, fables, parables, and proverbs. Many of the stories in this collection began as folk tales. Their ideals of courage, respect, responsibility, caring, and character represent the beauty in life which is more than skin-deep. These stories are landmarks in a developing culture of people. You can tell which values were important by the stories told in their time.

While writing this book, I learned that many storytellers, such as Æsop, never wrote down any of their stories. The stories were simply told over and over again, until they became woven into the fabric of the era. Old fairy tales and fables were collected by many writers, such as Joseph Jacobs and The Brothers Grimm, who took the time to preserve them in writing. Since the original authors are unknown, you will find these collections on the non-fiction shelves of public libraries. We knew few original authors, such as Hans Christian Andersen, whose fairy tales were written *before* their telling... and are therefore classified as fiction. Whether or not we know the origins of these stories, we owe a debt of gratitude to the many storytellers who passed them down throughout the ages. Our lives have been made richer by their wisdom.

I was raised on wisdom! The wisdom of these wonderful stories was handed down to me, the fourth generation storyteller. This wisdom is timeless, its moral value... powerfully significant. These stories have left their mark on my character... and my life. I wanted to do more than *tell* these stories to my own sons. I wanted to ensure their permanent place in our own family history. This legacy will help Aaron and Ben, someday, raise *their* children on rocking chair wisdom, too! It is with great passion, affection, and appreciation that I collected and recorded these stories *and* their life-changing lessons. From the rocking chair of the past, I claim them for today and tomorrow... for *all* of us.

Deb Austin Brown

*"There is nothing more sad or glorious
than generations changing hands."*

– John Cougar Mellencamp
singer, songwriter

Maw Great & Deb Brown

Part 1

WISDOM LEARNED
AT MAW GREAT'S KNEE...

Lesson One

Actions Speak Louder Than Words!

My great grandmother was born in 1881. She was a special person and a wonderful storyteller. Some of my favorite memories of her are rocking chair moments— times when I would sit in her lap and listen to stories. At the end of her stories, she would always say, "And the moral of the story is..." I could never get enough of her rocking chair wisdom.

Today, her rocking chair sits in the kitchen of my own home. The arms still display my own childhood teethmarks, where I would look up over the arms of her chair, begging for "just **one** more story!" I never had the heart to sand away those teethmarks. They are a reminder of the morals and values cut into my very character by the stories told from that chair. Maw Great would pick me up, put me on her lap, and begin rocking her way into a good story. She would spin the tales that began weaving the very fabric of my childhood. I cut more than my teeth on those old stories. Those stories put me to sleep at night, bonded me to my great grandmother, soothed sadness, let me know I was loved, and gave me a strong foundation for the values, habits, and character that have shaped my life.

Everyone loves a good story. There have been many storytellers throughout history who have put their pens to paper to forever capture a story that would live on in the hearts of readers throughout the ages. The fairy tales and fables of Æsop, The Brothers Grimm, Joseph Jacobs, Charles Perrault, and Hans Christian Andersen have traveled through generations, making their way from laps to legends. These storytellers and their stories have crafted the morals of the human spirit for scores of years. They teach the simplest truths of rocking chair wisdom. Rereading these fairy tales and fables as an adult is akin to a trip into the past— a revisiting of my great grandmother's attic, where new-found treasures of the past await this now-grown girl.

Today from the rocking chair we'll open a cherished collection of *Æsop's Fables.* This was one of Maw Great's favorites. Each story was short and to the point, with a moral teaching that would linger in your mind long after the story ended. Æsop was a Phrygian slave who lived around the 6th Century, B.C. Just like Uncle Remus, Æsop told his best stories about birds and beasts. His animal stories are built on the firm foundations of common sense and integrity that are very much a part of the human element. These fables have helped generations of children have moral ropes to hang on to when contemplating childhood decisions and actions. The repetition of these rocking chair lessons cut deliberate teethmarks into our very characters.

In his fable, *The Crab and His Mother,* Æsop tells the story of an old crab asking her son why he walks sideways. She continues on to tell him that he should always walk straight. The young crab replied, "Show me how, dear mother, and I'll follow your example." Of course, the old crab tried and tried in vain, and then saw how foolish she had been to find fault with her child. Æsop's adage: *"Example is better than precept."* As Maw Great would say, "The moral of the story is: *Showing is a more powerful teacher than telling.*"

As school bells ring out and children pour through classroom doors for the start of another school year, children everywhere will be introduced to new stories and new teachers. Around the world, teachers will become unbidden role models for their students. As teachers and parents, let us remember that modeling is the most powerful teacher. If we pay attention, our children will teach us a thing or two about the power of example.

Rocking Chair Wisdom: *Remember the powerful lesson of example. Your children will listen to what you say, but they will copy what you do! So, let positive example be your trademark!*

Believe You Can... And You Will!

No childhood is ever complete without the reading of bedtime stories. We all have memories of our favorite stories— the ones that we could never hear often enough, the ones that always ended with, "P-l-e-a-s-e, read it just **one** more time!" From the edge of a featherbed, from the front porch swing, and from great grandmother's rocking chair— stories have been told for generations. And we never tire of hearing them.

Stories have become a part of our heritage, a part of who we are. One of the most loved childhood stories is *The Tortoise and the Hare*. That turtle and rabbit have raced their way into almost everyone's childhood.

Æsop's fable begins in the forest with the Hare making fun of the Tortoise, "What a slow-poke you are! How do you expect to get anywhere at that rate? Why don't you pick up your heels and make some speed?" The Tortoise replied with confidence, "I'll run you a race and beat you any day." "Oho! If you are so anxious for a beating, my friend, I'll take you on tomorrow. In the meantime, I advise you to spend some time getting yourself in condition," taunted the Hare.

The next day, all the animals assembled to watch the contest. At the signal, the runners were off; the Tortoise at his usual slow gait, the Hare speeding far ahead. But having run half of the agreed distance, with the Tortoise far behind, the Hare thought, "What a joke! That fellow will never catch up with me. I'll just take a little nap, and trot along to the goal later."

So he lay down and slept. But the Tortoise, slowly and tirelessly jogged on, never stopping; he passed the sleeping Hare, and steadily continued towards the goal. The Hare finally awakened and sped up to the goalpost only to find that the Tortoise, amid the cheers of the spectators, had won the race. Æsop's adage: *"Slow and steady wins the race."* And as Maw Great would say, "The moral of the story is: ***Believe in yourself and your abilities.***"

I think back to those rocking chair days of my youth when my great grandmother would tell me how special I was. She told me and showed me so frequently that it became natural for me to believe it. Maw Great's belief in me transcended grandmotherly boundaries to my own perceptions. Because she was able to believe in me, I came to believe in myself. And there was great power in it!

Belief in self is a prerequisite to any achievement and success in life. Napoleon Hill and W. Clement Stone's writings have taught us that we can, indeed, *believe and achieve*! Once formed, a child's belief in self is very difficult to change. So, there are only two choices for the children in our lives: a positive belief in self... or a life filled with self-doubt.

Positive tortoises achieve their goals. Their focus is sharp and determined, and they are relentless in their pursuit. They aren't distracted by the opinions and qualifications of others. Their strong belief in self propels them onward. They may travel at a slower pace, at times, but they do arrive at the finish line—punctually and proudly. Deep down, they always believe they can, and they never stop to rest until their goal is reached!

As parents and teachers, it is our job to believe in our children until they can believe in themselves. It is our responsibility to help our children get into condition for the races of life. The future of each runner depends on it!

Rocking Chair Wisdom: *Belief in self is the foundation for all eventual success in life. That belief will help cheer you on to the finish lines of life!*

Lesson Three

Be The Little Engine That... Can!

As fall breezes usher this cool November evening to a close, I pick a book from the shelf and head for my great grandmother's rocking chair. Outside the window, the sun begins its descent behind hills painted in autumn splendor. Even Crayola could not master the brilliance of these leaves and trees!

This evening I choose the red storybook with the soft, worn edges. It is a well-read book, loved into Realness like the Velveteen Rabbit from Storybook Land. As I leaf through the frayed pages, I come across an unfamiliar fable by Æsop. *The Donkey, the Cock, and the Lion* is one fable missed in my childhood, so today's reading is my first.

As the story goes, a Lion prowled past a prosperous farmyard one evening, and saw a fat Donkey. "My dinner!" he rejoiced, and crouched for the spring. The Donkey was so afraid that he froze with fear. At that very moment, the Rooster in the barnyard began to crow the end of day. The raucous noise startled the Lion, who turned and ran off as fast as his legs would carry him.

The Donkey, instead of leaving well enough alone, thought he would turn the situation to his own advantage. He ran after the retreating Lion at a great pace, calling to everyone to notice how the King of Beasts had fled before him. Suddenly the Lion, having fully recovered from his fright, wheeled around— and that was the end of the Donkey! Æsop's adage: ***"Over-confidence often ends in ruin."*** As Maw Great would say: ***"Don't get too big for your britches."***

Self-confidence is a wonderful thing. It is a necessary and needed character trait. Without it, the fragile human spirit is broken and life is less than it should be. We've all seen the kind of cocky arrogance that tends to give confidence a bad name. The Donkey displayed it well. And on the other hand, we've all seen the kind of devastation that the lack of confidence can cause in the lives of unintentioned losers.

Remember the childhood story, *The Little Engine That Could*. That little engine's confidence made for a happy ending. We need to know that self confidence can pave the way for happy endings in our adventures, too.

The great motivators— Carnegie, Hill, Stone, Peale, Mitchell, Waitley, Covey, Schuller, Brown, Ziglar... have all written volumes on the importance of self-confidence. Les Brown's powerful book, *Live Your Dreams,* provides soul-stirring insights into the importance of self confidence. Dr. William Mitchell's book, *Winning in the Land of Giants,* is a wonderful work explicating the power of self-confidence in overcoming "grasshopper mentality". He reminds us that grass-hopper mentality will keep us from reaching our full potential, and that we can develop the confidence and courage of a "giant slayer" in our own "Land of Promise". Sure, we all face giants in our lives, giants that overwhelm us and freeze us in our tracks. And, from time to time, we all need a wake-up call from the Rooster in the barnyard!

It's never too late to tune-in to ourselves and our abilities. Self confidence can be achieved at any age. Just like the Lion, we can go on the prowl for what we need to feed our confidence. Associating with positive people, reading positive books and materials, and thinking in positive ways are all positively productive in building our self confidence. Learning to set goals and working diligently toward them will help us achieve small successes on which we can build confidence for the future. Remember that every great journey begins with a single step. When venturing out, personalize the question Dr. Robert Schuller asked, "What great thing would *you* attempt if you knew that you would not fail?"

Rocking Chair Wisdom: *Confidence in yourself and your abilities will help you stare down the Lions you'll face in the barnyards of life!*

Lesson Four

Expect A Magic Beanstalk!

Rocking chairs are wonderful places to spend cold winter mornings! The creaking sound takes me back to my great grandmother's house. The house was grand and magnificent, its eighteen rooms filled with the happiest of childhood memories. Maw Great's rocking chair sat on a handmade braided rug that stretched over beautiful hardwood floors. I remember the clock on the mantel chiming away the early daylight hours, as morning's first sunlight made its way through the kitchen window. How I miss those mornings on my great grandmother's farm!

This winter morning I'm reading Æsop's shortest fable. Three sentences tell the story of *The Mountain in Eruption.* Once with a mighty rumbling, a Mountain began to quake and tremble as if it would erupt. Thousands gathered to watch the phenomenon. At last, with a final tremendous heave, the Mountain split, and out of the cleft popped a little Mouse. Æsop's adage: ***"Mighty promise often brings small result."*** As Maw Great would say, ***"Things aren't always what they seem."***

It's true. If we stand back and watch, life doesn't always give us what we expect. In Æsop's tale, we expected more from that mountain. Could a little Mouse really have caused all of that rumbling? In Stephen Covey's book, *The Seven Habits of Highly Effective People,* he quotes Bruce Barton: "Sometimes when I consider what tremendous consequences come from little things... I am tempted to think... there are no little things." Æsop would obviously agree.

It has been said that we make our lives one day at a time; we make our character one act at a time. The little things add up resolutely to make the big things. Sometimes a seemingly insignificant act may be the most important thing you will do in forming your character. As Dr. William Mitchell has said, "We simply don't know which choices in life are the big ones." But we **can** expect that every choice we make will make a difference in who we become.

Expectations are an important part of life. They can set us up for failure or they can set us up for success. The choice is **yours**! It really **is** up to you! We usually get out of life just what we expect. Set your sights on higher aspirations, and the world is at your feet. Aim at nothing, and that is exactly what you'll get. Hockey-great Wayne Gretzsky warned, "We miss 100% of the shots we never take." It's a consistent no-win approach to life.

There are many storybook characters who had high expectations. Jack certainly was reaching for the sky when he traded the family cow for a handful of magic beans. His mother was so angry that she threw the beans out of the window. But Jack had great expectations. He certainly was not disappointed as he climbed the beanstalk to bigger and better things!

In the fairy tale, *The Three Little Pigs*, the third little pig had high expectations for his life, too. He secured his future by building wisely with bricks, ensuring a firm foundation for success... away from the big bad Wolf!

It's great news to know that you can write your own endings in life! Set your sights high, on things that really matter. Write down your goals and commit them to memory. Stay sharp and focused. Then the small choices you make in life will all add up... in big ways!

Rocking Chair Wisdom: Unleash the power of an erupting mountain by setting high expectations for yourself and your life. Remember, you'll only get what you expect and work for. It's a self-fulling prophecy!

Lesson Five

Goal Setting
Gives Shape To Your Dreams!

A new year dawns as an old year is torn from the calendar pages. Traditionally, the start of a new year triggers a list of New Year's Resolutions. Well-intentioned people take a closer look at their habits, making amends in the less-than-strong areas of their lives.

Thinking back to the rocking chair days of my youth, I remember the wisdom of my great grandmother. The longer she rocked in that chair, the more good advice she dished out. How I wish she were here today to help me during times of doubt! But, those long years ago, she gave me the tools I would need in every stage of my life.

One of the things I learned from her was the valuable wisdom of setting goals. Not just on New Year's Day, but *each* day, it's critical to review and establish goals. That's the only way to become productive, Maw Great would say.

As I sit in her rocking chair today, I feel connected to the past. Although it's been almost thirty years since Maw Great died, I can *hear* her voice of encouragement. From the time I was five years old, she helped me learn to establish my priorities and set to work. Along the way I learned that goals are wonderful to achieve, but that the journey to them is what gives life its real substance. Actress Bette Davis once said that she hoped her children would learn that ***"the working for it... is what brings the real joy."*** That's the same lesson my great grandmother taught me. It's one of life's purest truths.

One of the tales that Maw Great read to me often was Æsop's *The Crow and the Pitcher.* As Æsop explained, a Crow who was desperate with thirst could find no water anywhere except at the bottom of an old pitcher in a deserted garden. Although he stretched and strained, the water level was so low that he could not reach it. He tried to break the pitcher, but it was too strong. He tried to overturn it, but it was too heavy. At last, he devised the following plan: with great patience he dropped many little pebbles one by one into the water, until it was raised far enough so that he could drink. Æsop's adage: ***"Little by little does the trick."*** As Maw Great would say: ***"If you want something badly enough, you can find a way to make it happen."***

Think of how important goals are in sports. Whether it is the net in soccer, the end zone in football, the hole in golf, or the hoop in basketball— the athlete must have a focus for his play. Practice is the key. As Dr. William Mitchell always says, "Application, application, application!" Tony Robbins reinforces, "repetition is the mother of skill." Great coaches all know the importance of daily goal setting in coaching their players to victory. Goal setting will help *you* on the playing field of life!

Geoffrey F. Albert said, "The most important thing about goals is having one." Napoleon Hill and W. Clement Stone devoted their lives and their writings to the importance of having goals. Those of us fortunate enough to have attended a Power of Positive Students Workshop with Dr. Mitchell, have participated in a Goal Setting Workshop. Research tells the whole story: 87% of people do not have goals; 10% of people have goals; and 3% of people have *written* goals. Those who set goals in writing achieve 50 to 100 times *more* than those who fail to commit their goals in writing! So, think about what you want to achieve in life, and... start writing!

Goal setting is the place where your dreams begin to take shape. So, harness the power! ***Goal setting provides you the compass for navigating through life.*** It will keep you in the company of the stars! And, the sky really will be the limit.

Rocking Chair Wisdom: *Be a member of the 3% Club! Set goals and commit them to writing. The rest will be history!*

Lesson Six

Teamwork
Is The Best Work!

After a long winter, a change of season is as timely as a breath of fresh air. I remember spring at my great grandmother's house. Everything was green with promise. The cows grazed in nearby fields, rabbits hopped along wooden fences, and ponies frolicked together in play. Watching nature in the springtime always made me feel truly alive!

My great grandmother's house had three porches— all complete with ferns, rocking chairs, and porch swings. My sister, Ellen, and I traveled many miles on those porch swings. In the afternoons, Maw Great would join us for talks, laughter, and together-time. Bowl on her lap, she would string beans, shuck corn, or peel apples while she talked. It wasn't long before she was off on a good story.

Like Æsop, Maw Great used nature in her stories. From her we learned about life, the difference between right and wrong, and how to get along with people. Æsop has a myriad of fables about the importance of getting along with others. It has often been said, and sung, ***"United we stand; divided we fall."*** Æsop's tale about *The Bulls and the Lion* illustrates this message well.

Four Bulls were greatly threatened by a savage Lion who hunted in the neighborhood. They decided to form a league for mutual protection. "If we just stick together," they said, "no Lion will dare to attack us." So for a time, they grazed together in the same meadow, and the prowling Lion began to give up hope. But soon, the Bulls fell into an argument. They separated, each departing in anger to another meadow. The Lion was able to attack them one by one, and so gained his end. Æsop's adage: ***"There is strength in unity, weakness in division."*** As Maw Great would say: ***"It's better to stick together."***

Æsop has another fable about the power of teamwork, *The Bundle of Sticks.* A farmer had three sons who were always quarreling among themselves. The farmer loved them deeply and was distressed about their constant bickering. He also feared for the security of his land after his death. To teach his sons the impor-

of sticking together, he bade them to go into the woods and collect a large number of sticks. He bundled them together and tied them firmly.

The farmer had each of his sons try to break the bundle of sticks. Of course, no one could. Then, the farmer untied the bundle, and separated the sticks. Giving each son a single stick, he said, "Now try to break them." The sons had little difficulty breaking these sticks. Astonished, the sons asked their father why he had them to do this.

"To teach you a lesson," replied the father. "As long as you three men remain together, each one supporting the others, you are a match for all who try to harm you. But as soon as you separate, you can be broken as easily as these single sticks!" Æsop's adage: *"Strength lies in union."* As Maw Great would say again: *"It's still better to stick together."*

Robert Fulghum said it well, too, in his book, *All I Really Needed to Know I Learned in Kindergarten*: *"It is still true, no matter how old you are— when you go out into the world, it is best to hold hands and stick together."*

These long years later, Ellen and I are still growing in that rocking chair wisdom. And we still believe that it's better to stick together!

Rocking Chair Wisdom: *In nature, in families, and in the world— it's better to stick together. Teamwork is always the best work!*

Say What You Mean... Mean What You Say!

My great grandmother loved me! She communicated that to me in lots of ways— she loved me with her words and deeds, because she loved me with her attitude. She was always glad to see our family-packed station wagon come up the long driveway to her farmhouse. As soon as we saw her come through the screen door, the smiles started. Then came the hugs, kisses, and laughter! I could see, hear, and feel her love for me!

Communication is so important. It gives life to any relationship! And when it's flowing smoothly, the quality of our life improves remarkably. Stress levels are low, and energy levels are high. All is right with the world!

Æsop's often-quoted fable, *The Shepherd's Boy and the Wolf,* is a childhood classic. From the porch swing, the kitchen table, and the rocking chair— Maw Great told this one...over, and over, and over! In fact, I always thought the name of this fable was *The Little Boy Who Cried Wolf.* A Shepherd Boy was tending his flock near a village and thought it would be great fun to hoax the villagers by pretending that a Wolf was attacking the sheep; so he shouted out, "Wolf! Wolf!" When the villagers came running to assist the boy, he laughed at them for their efforts. He did this more than once, and each time the villagers found that a trick had been played on them, for there was no Wolf at all.

At last a Wolf really did come, and the Boy cried, "Wolf! Wolf!" as loudly as he could. The people of the village were so used to his tricks that no one took notice of his cries for help. And so the Wolf had it his own way and killed off sheep after sheep, with no one to stop him. Æsop's adage: ***"You cannot believe a liar even when he tells the truth."*** As Maw Great would say: ***"Say what you mean, and mean what you say."***

The Little Boy sent a message to the people of his village. The message was one of inconsideration and disrespect. He communicated it with his words; he communicated it with his deeds. Most importantly, he communicated it with his attitude. He lost in big ways— he lost the trust of his friends and neighbors.

When Maw Great sat in her rocking chair and told me stories, she communicated her love for me. Her attitude was inviting and loving. She really didn't have to say anything to get me up into her lap. I *knew* that she wanted me there!

We need to remember that we communicate with our looks, gestures, body language, attitude, voice, *and* words. Say what you mean, and mean what you say. The quality of your relationships depend on it!

In his fables, Æsop communicated many messages to us. He spent his life communicating the knowledge, feelings, and values that he felt were important. His inner voice told him that his work would somehow make the world a better place.

Truth is universal. Whether fables really began with Æsop or Adam, we have cherished the values of these teachings for thousands of years. Our lives have been made better from the readings. This rocking chair wisdom has guided children down moral paths for generations. Æsop saw to it; he ensured it with his teachings. He taught us one moral for life— and that moral is truth. G.K. Chesterton wrote of Æsop's stories: "There is every type and kind of fable; but there is one moral to the fable, because there is only one moral to everything."

Rocking Chair Wisdom: *Remember the little boy who cried "Wolf!" Say what you mean, and mean what you say.*

Lesson Eight

Bend...
So You Don't Break!

May is a beautiful month! The air is so fragrant, and the grass and trees are such a beautiful green. My great grandmother's yard was filled with trees— big ones. Many trees were older than the house itself, which was built before the Civil War. Stately and tall, these were trees to build hopes on. Many days during my childhood, I rested in their shade, tablet and pencil in hand, to record my thoughts. At the foot of these trees, I got my start as a writer.

Throughout time, trees have been an important part of nature. Children have climbed them, lovers have carved their initials in the bark, and visionaries have looked up through their branches to dream. Trees give shade, shelter, oxygen, and wood. They also furnish us with insight about the changes and seasons in life. For Æsop, trees provided kindling for more stories.

The fable *The Olive Tree and the Fig Tree* hands us a life-lesson on coping. An Olive tree teased a Fig tree with the loss of her leaves at a certain season of year. "You," she said, "lose your leaves every autumn, and are bare until the spring: whereas I, you see, remain green and flourishing all the year round."

Soon afterwards there came a heavy fall of snow, which settled on the leaves of the Olive so heavily that she broke under the weight; but the flakes fell harmlessly through the bare branches of the Fig, which survived to bear many more crops. Æsop's adage: ***"Don't let life's problems weigh you down."*** As Maw Great would say: ***"Bend, so you don't break."***

The Fig tree had a positive attitude about her branches. She was prepared for the snowfall, and therefore was able to cope with winter's delivery. The Olive tree let the accumulation of snow get her down. She let the burden accumulate until it reached unmanageable proportions. Finally, she broke under the pressure. A single snowflake cannot cause an avalanche, but many flakes together can cause much trouble. It's a rocking chair lesson worth learning.

For a long time, I had trouble with hair dryers. My father became the repairman for the ones that I shorted out, burned up, and ruined. Every few months, I would take him the newest casualty. Tired of the constant repairs and the expense of new dryers, I asked *why* I had so much trouble with them. Dad showed me the little mesh wire cover that collects the dust and protects the motor. Now I understand the need for a little preventative maintenance. Every few weeks, I take a pair of tweezers and remove the lint. The motor no longer overheats and burns out. It's that simple.

The lint in life does tend to accumulate until it causes problems of larger proportions. All is takes is a little forethought and planning to avoid potential problems. After all, **"An ounce of prevention is worth a pound of cure!"**

Even sidewalks are built for coping with the stresses and strains of life. Construction workers put spaces in the concrete every few feet to help relieve pressure. This wise planning keeps the sidewalk from cracking under the pressures of day to day use. We need to put spaces in our lives, too, to help *us* avoid cracking under pressure.

Flexibility is an arborescent quality that will help us bend so we will not break under the pressures of life. Like trees, we need to learn to sway in the breezes, winds, and storms of life. Your positive attitude will act like sunshine to melt away the problem snow on your own branches!

Rocking Chair Wisdom: *Positive attitudes are the roots that will help you stand strong and treelike during the winds and storms of life. Plant wisely... and stand your ground!*

Lesson Nine

You Can Go A Long Way After You Are Tired!

My great grandmother was strong... and determined. She lived at the turn of the twentieth century, when feminine strength was less than newsworthy. Maw Great was a woman of quiet courage and confidence. She faced life's challenges head-on with obduracy and a positive attitude. She believed that *anything* could be accomplished with hard work and sacrifice. And because she believed it and lived it, I came to believe it, too. I've lived my life knowing it, and my life has been the better for it.

The rocking chair was Maw Great's trademark. She had several in her stately Kentucky farmhouse. At the head of her long, wooden farmtable in the kitchen sat her most-used rocking chair. Late in the evening, she could be found there wearing her Cincinnati Reds baseball cap, cheering for her favorite team on the radio. Sometimes I'd join her as she listened. We'd talk for nine full innings. Maw Great used those baseball evenings to teach me the value of physical conditioning, practice, sacrifice, hard work... and teamwork. It was at her knee that I fell in love with sports! She taught me to respect and appreciate the challenges of the game. It was my great grandmother who bought me my first baseball cap. I wore it from the time I was four years old. These many years later, I still like to wear a ball cap, and I still think of her when I pull my long hair through the back of it. I remember the fun, the love, and the wisdom of that rich and wonderful heritage...from the rocking chair days of my youth!

My great grandmother used stories to illustrate her conversations with me. There was always a lesson to be learned. Her favorite stories were fables, fairy tales, and proverbs. One French proverb that illustrates her life is: ***"One may go a long way after one is tired."*** I like this one so much, that I keep it taped to the top of my computer monitor. I refer to it often because it's such a powerful life-lesson. As Maw Great would say: ***"Dig down deep inside yourself and find the strength you need."***

My great grandmother lived that lesson. She got up every morning with the roosters, and worked hard all day long. She never complained— she just stayed busy with running a home, tending a garden, caring for the farm animals, and running a dairy and tobacco farm. In the course of a day she cooked three hot meals, baked pies, cleaned house, washed laundry and ironed, picked and canned vegetables from the garden, gathered eggs from the henhouse, killed and plucked a chicken or two for the evening meal, sewed her own clothes, crocheted bedspreads and afghans, had a friend over for afternoon tea, read books, kept up with world news, watered her beautiful ferns, took a walk, put me in her lap for a good story, cuddled with us kids on the porch swing, and played a game of baseball in the side yard. There was always lots of hard work... but there was always love, laughter, and fun! Looking back on it, I realize that she had a perfectly balanced life. I marvel at the miraculous simplicity of it!

Today's world is so different. We're living life in the fast lane, and burn-out levels are at an all-time high. Stress is the name of the game. Families are on the go! Families now have full-time jobs, kids involved in several sports, and dinner in the drive-thru lane. Is anyone even at home in America before seven o'clock in the evening? Are there any children at the knee of a caring adult listening to the rocking chair wisdom of old? Where have all the stories gone?

Today's life presents challenges that Maw Great never knew. But now-grown kids raised on rocking chair wisdom are ready for those challenges. Like the athlete who constantly presses-on in competition, they rise to meet the demands of the day. Tune-in to the wisdom! Keep your sense of humor, enjoy each and every day. Balance your life with work, play, laughter, and love. And remember to share some rocking chair wisdom with the children in *your* life!

Rocking Chair Wisdom: *Believe in yourself! You can go a long way after you are tired. Dig down deep inside yourself and find the strength that is there. It's a life-challenge you can meet head-on with rocking chair wisdom!*

Dare To Dream!

It was a favorite part of my childhood. In the summer, we would travel to Kentucky to visit my great grandmother. As soon as we turned into the long driveway of her magnificent home, I knew I had it made! This was a farm that I could get lost on!

Being from a family of eight, it was sometimes difficult to find a place for just me— a place and time to daydream. But, here on Maw Great's farm, I had it made! There was lots of together-time, but I could also enjoy some much-needed solitude. It was in her sprawling front yard that I'd lose myself... usually at the foot of one of the tall and stately oak trees. I'd pack-up the afternoon necessities— tablet, pencil, a few warm peanut butter cookies, and some fresh-squeezed lemonade— and head for the great outdoors, alone. Ah-h! The simple wonder of it all!

It was during these special times that I could indulge myself in one of my favorite pasttimes... daydreaming. It's one of the grand luxuries of life! But don't be fooled. It's also one of life's great *necessities!*

Think of some of the storybook characters whose dreams led to storybook magic. Jack was tired of his meager existence and dreamed of finding a better life for himself and his mother. His daydreams laid the foundation for the risk-taking of trading the family cow for a fistful of magic beans. His mother was a non-believer; but Jack, nonetheless, climbed his way to wonderful places in the sky! Cinderella took the time to daydream, too. While mopping the floor and doing the chores, she dreamed of going to the ball. She dreamed of wearing a beautiful gown and dancing with the prince. Her step-sisters laughed at the foolishness of her dream. The power of dreaming afforded Cinderella a perfect fit with her new life... with the prince!

Happily-ever-after doesn't just happen in Storybook Land. ***Good things happen in real life because real people, like you and me, dare to dream!*** Maw Great taught me that. It was part of her rocking chair wisdom.

At the foot of the grand old oaks, I did my share of daydreaming. I dreamed of big things and small things... I let my imagination run wild. I spent time getting to know myself— my innermost thoughts, needs, and feelings. It was during these times that I charted my future. Nothing would stand in the way of my dreams! The lessons I had learned on self-respect, hard work, sacrifice, and determination would carry me through.

Today's children are bombarded with things to do and places to go. They are involved with after-school sports, social events, and recreational activities. They spend time in their bedrooms talking on the phone, listening to music, playing computer or video games, and watching television. Little time, if any, is left for daydreaming, self-discovery, or goal setting. Perhaps a little trip to the foot of an oak tree is in order.

Parents and teachers can set the example. Leaving time within the day for solitude and reflection is a way to ensure that the children in your life will come to understand the importance of taking time to dream. Share a little of yourself with them— your thoughts, feelings, and dreams. It will give them a starting place for getting to know themselves.

Dreams are a product of time and opportunity alone. Take time for yourself at the foot of a towering oak. Daydreaming is powerful, indeed! Please don't miss out on the adventure!

Rocking Chair Wisdom: *Reach for your future... dare to dream! All great successes in life start from the seed of a daydream. There is a great oak in your future!*

Hard Work
Never Hurt Anyone!

On a typical day on the farm, my great grandmother put in a full day of hard work. It never hurt her, either. In fact, she seemed to thrive on it! The more Maw Great busied herself with hard work, the happier she seemed to be. Over the years I heard her say many times, **"Hard work never hurt anyone."** Now I catch myself saying it to my own sons and to the students in my class. It's a priceless bit of rocking chair wisdom.

There are many storybook tales that illustrate the importance of hard work. Browsing through the story of *The Three Little Pigs*, we see the power of doing a job well. A half-hearted effort with inferior materials left little competition for the big bad Wolf. Hard work and attention to detail definitely paid off for the third little pig. Even his brothers appreciated the shelter that a solid effort provided. The hard work of the third little pig blew the competition away! The third little pig worked smarter than his brothers. He lived securely in the brick house... away from the big bad Wolf!

In the story of *The Little Red Hen,* we see another example of hard work. Obviously, hard work never hurt the cat, the dog, or the duck. When the little red hen solicited help for her garden, no one was interested in the project. They sat back and watched as the little red hen planted, tended, cut, milled, baked, and ate! She enjoyed the fruits of her labor... alone. The cat, dog, and duck sat back and watched as the little red hen worked hard. They also sat back and watched as she ate the delicious fresh-baked bread!

In Æsop's fable *Hercules and the Wagoner*, we see an example of a wagoner waiting for someone else to come along and do his work for him. A wagoner was driving his team along a muddy road, pulling a full load. The wagon wheels sank so deeply into the mud that the horses could not pull the wagon out. As he stood there, looking helplessly on, the wagoner called out to Hercules for help. The god appeared to him and said, "Put your shoulder to the wheel and goad on your horses, before you call on Hercules to assist you. If you won't lift a finger to help yourself, you can't expect Hercules or anyone else to come to your aid." Æsop's adage: ***"Heaven helps those who help themselves."*** As Maw Great would say again: ***"Hard work never hurt anyone."***

Æsop has another fable to enlighten us, *The Farmer and His Sons*. A farmer, who was near death, called his sons to his deathbed. "My sons, I am shortly about to die. I want for you to know that in my vineyard lies a hidden treasure. Dig, and you shall find it."

As soon as their father was dead, the sons took shovels and began turning up the soil of the vineyard over and over again, in search of the hidden treasure which was supposed to be buried there. They found no hidden treasure. The vines, after so thorough a digging, produced a crop such as had never before been seen. Æsop's hidden message: ***"There is no treasure without toil."*** As Maw Great would echo: ***"Hard work never hurt anyone!"***

Think about your own life. It's true that you feel best when you put in a good day's work and are productive. Laziness never inspires anyone to be happier. Modeling hard work and its rewards is a wonderful way to teach the children in your life about the hidden treasures that are reaped by hard work!

Rocking Chair Wisdom: *Dig for the treasure! Balance your life with work and play. Remember, hard work never hurt anyone!*

Lesson Twelve

Honesty
Is The Best Policy!

Honesty is the best policy. This bit of rocking chair wisdom has been passed on for generations and generations. It's an axiom that we all know by heart. People, like my great grandmother, saw to it by telling their rocking chair stories of old... over, and over, and over.

There are many characters, fictional and real, whose names are synonymous with honesty and its antithesis. George Washington, Pinocchio, Honest Abe Lincoln, The Little Boy Who Never Told a Lie, Benjamin Franklin, and The Little Boy Who Cried Wolf— all are well-known for their honesty or lack of it. Their decisions regarding honesty set them apart from the crowd. Storytellers, over the years, have made their legends a part of everyone's childhood.

The story of *Pinocchio,* perhaps, best illustrates the consequences of not telling the truth. Carlo Lorenzini's classic nineteenth-century Italian tale gives us an instantly recognizable symbol of dishonesty. Pinocchio had fallen in with the wrong crowd, and was given to stretching the truth. Each time that he told a lie, his wooden nose grew. As is the usual case with lies, the situation had gotten out of hand. Finally, Pinocchio's nose had grown so long that he could not exit the door. The Fairy looked at him and began to laugh at all of the foolish lies he had told. Pinocchio responded, "How did you know that they were lies?" "Lies, my boy," said the Fairy, "are recognized at once because they are of only two kinds. Some have short legs, and others have long noses." The Fairy let Pinocchio suffer the consequences and cry for a while so that he would learn his lesson. But when she saw his eyes swollen and his face red from weeping, she was moved by pity to action. She summoned a flock of woodpeckers, who flew in the window and perched on Pinocchio's nose. They pecked away until his nose was restored to its original size.

Hopefully, we won't have to go through such a traumatic situation to learn the lesson of honesty. But it's important to know what Maw Great taught me, ***"Lies always get out of hand!"*** When one lie is told, many others become necessary in order to cover up the original. The consequences are always of the long-nosed variety. They are hard to hide. ***We wear lies on our character as plain as the nose on Pinocchio's face!***

The chopping down of the cherry tree is probably the most famous legend about honesty in all of America. Young George owned up to his mistake right away, becoming a role model for children everywhere. His father was proud of his courage and honesty, putting the welfare of his cherry orchard second to the moral rearing of his son. George Washington never forgot the message of that day. His life was lived in an honest and honorable way. The seeds were planted that day in the orchard with his father.

In the fairy tale, *The Frog Prince,* the king's daughter had promised her love and caring to whoever would retrieve her ball from the royal pond. Little did she expect that the frog would hold her to her promise. When she tried to renege, the king insisted that his daughter keep her promise, no matter how odd it seemed. The princess finally said, "Father is right; I must keep my promise." She took the frog in and put him on a royal pillow, catering to his every need. The princess was rewarded for her honesty when the frog turned into a handsome prince. They, of course, lived happily ever after in Storybook Land... proving that great rewards come to those who are true to their word.

The rewards for honesty aren't always as dramatic as *happily ever after*. But nothing is more satisfying than the intrinsically wonderful feeling of knowing that you've done the right thing. So, as Maw Great would say, ***"Dig down deep inside yourself and find the strength to do the right thing."*** Honesty *is* the best policy!

Rocking Chair Wisdom: Truthfulness is one of the marks of great character. It's something that will set you apart from the rest of the crowd. Live happily ever after... with honesty as your policy!

Lesson Thirteen

Be A Friend...
So You Can Have A Friend!

"Once upon a time..." is a great beginning for the stories that have trademarked our childhoods. At the knee of a caring adult, children through the generations have listened intently to the storybook tales of youth, learning the moral lessons of their wisdom. The repetition of these stories has given each generation moral ropes to hang onto during the choice-times of childhood... and beyond.

Going to my great grandmother's farm was a cherished childhood event. But one drawback to those trips was having no friends there to play with. Socially, I was cut off from hometown friends my own age. My friends were two hundred miles away. And for a young school-age girl, it might as well have been a million miles! So, when I returned home from Kentucky, I was thrilled to be with my friends again! It was a lesson I learned at an early age, about appreciating those friendships and not taking them for granted.

Maw Great taught me that *friendship is the noblest profession, and that the best way to have a friend is to be a friend.* Hundreds of authors have written on the subject of friendship. Those stories illustrate the basic need in all of us to have and to be a friend.

In their fairy tale, *The Cat and Mouse in Partnership,* The Brothers Grimm wrote of the disappointment and disaster that can come from choosing the wrong friend. A cat and a mouse became such good friends that they decided to set up housekeeping together. "We must make provision for the winter, or we shall go hungry," said the cat. So together they decided to store a pot of honey under the church altar to save for colder, hungrier times. The cat was a dishonest friend and, on several occasions, sneaked there under the pretense of good... to dip into the honey pot. Finally, all of the honey was gone. As the mouse discovered the betrayal, the cat pounced upon her and thus caused her end.

We've all known the hurt that can come from a disappointing friendship; the emotional scars can be long-lasting. But, sometimes in life, we are treated to a wonderful, fulfilling friendship…where the rewards are heartwarming, indeed. It is such a relationship that illustrates friendship in its best light.

Perhaps the most-loved story about real friendship is the one by Margery Williams. *The Velveteen Rabbit* is one of my childhood favorites. It is a story that Maw Great read to me, and one that I reread often as an adult. It is the story about friendship in the truest sense of the word— the story about how toys become Real.

A young boy found the velveteen rabbit in his stocking on Christmas morning. At first, the rabbit lived in the nursery along with the other toys. The skin horse, who had been loved into Realness, shared his nursery wisdom: "Real isn't how you are made…it's a thing that happens to you. It doesn't happen all at once. You become. Generally, by the time you are Real, most of your hair has been loved off… and you become very shabby. Once you become Real, you can't be ugly, except to people who don't understand." The velveteen rabbit longed for nursery magic to make him Real, too.

Over time, the rabbit became the boy's favorite toy— playing in the yard by day, and sleeping with the boy every night. When the boy came down with a case of scarlet fever, the doctor insisted that the stuffed rabbit be thrown out in the trash, in an effort to rid the boy's bedroom of germs. The velveteen rabbit felt as though his heart would break. Outside in the garbage sack that night, he cried a real tear. And out of that tear, stepped a beautiful fairy. "I am the nursery magic fairy. I take care of all the toys that children have loved. I take them with me and turn them into Real." The little rabbit's dream came true… he was loved into becoming Real!

For generations, the story of this sawdust-filled rabbit has touched the hearts of young and old, alike. It is the story of friendship in the purest form, a marvel in today's ever-disposable society. As Maw Great would say, "The Girl Scout song may hold the needed lesson, here: ***Make new friends but keep the old: one is silver, the other gold.***"

Rocking Chair Wisdom: Friendship is a noble profession, one that will enrich your life in wonderful ways. Remember the rocking chair story of the velveteen rabbit. Having and being a friend is the real way to a happier life!

Lesson Fourteen

Love Makes The World Go 'Round!

Storybooks contain the fairy tales and historic epics of old, and many of them grant us insight into romance throughout the ages. I'll have to admit: I'm a romantic at heart. Stories of true love, whether fictional or real, have always touched my heart. From the rocking chair, my great grandmother taught me that **love is, indeed, a wonderful thing!** As I snuggled close under Maw Great's chin, her stories had me begging for more. I was always a sucker for a happy ending!

From Germany, comes the story of *Rapunzel* penned by The Brothers Grimm. It was one of my childhood favorites. Rapunzel was the most beautiful child in the world! When she was twelve years old, the old witch shut Rapunzel up in a tower in the midst of a wood. The witch kept her in the tower alone for many years. Only the witch could enter the tower by calling out, "Rapunzel, Rapunzel, let down your hair." The witch would then climb Rapunzel's long, golden locks to reach the tiny window at the top of the tower.

One day, the king's son was riding through the woods and heard a voice singing so sweetly that he stopped to listen. He tried to get Rapunzel out of his mind, but her sweet song had captured his heart. He tried to get into the tower to see Rapunzel, but the witch tricked him— and he fell from the tall tower. The prince escaped with his life, but the thorny thicket into which he fell scratched out his eyes. He spent his days wandering the woods blindly, lamenting the loss of his dear Rapunzel.

Many miserable years later, the king's son wandered upon a deserted place in the wood and heard the sweet, familiar voice of the maiden he still loved. Rapunzel knew him immediately and fell into his arms, weeping. When her tears touched his eyes, they became clear again, and he could see! He took Rapunzel to his kingdom, where they were received with great joy, and there they lived..."happily ever after."

From France we have two well-loved fairy tales, collected by Charles Perrault: *Cinderella* and *Sleeping Beauty*. These are two of the most romantic stories found between the pages of a book. In the first story, we see an example of the rags-to-riches existence of a young girl turned princess. With the help of her fairy godmother, Cinderella received a royal welcome at the ball. The prince fell in love with her at first sight! He had to try the glass slipper on many feet before he found his one, true love. But, the prince was determined. Only Cinderella proved to be the perfect fit! It was another case of *happily ever after*. And I was happy to hear this childhood favorite over and over again!

In the tale of *Sleeping Beauty*, we have the tender story of a beautiful young girl who was christened with six wonderful blessings and one curse. The curse foretold that if she were pricked and her finger did bleed, that she would sleep for one hundred years. As hard as the king tried, he could not help the curse from coming true. He placed his sleeping daughter on a beautiful bed and protected her in a secluded place. A hundred years later, the new king's son found her, kissed her, and brought her back to life. She knew that this was the prince she had been waiting for all of her life. Good had triumphed over evil in this happy storybook ending!

Maw Great always said, ***"To love and to be loved is the greatest joy on earth!"*** And I have learned from a dear friend, Betty, never to be ashamed to have real feelings for someone. Those are two powerful lessons in romance! From the rocking chair of the past... I pass them on.

***Rocking Chair Wisdom:** Whether in real life or in storybooks, love does make the world go 'round! To give and receive love is the greatest joy on earth! Never be ashamed to have real feelings for someone. Love is always a risk worth taking. It's the only way to find your own happy ending!*

Lesson Fifteen

You Can't Buy Wisdom
In The Five And Dime!

Every Saturday we would go! It was the highlight of the weekend. Summer, autumn, winter, spring... it was always the same. We'd walk to the bottom of College Hill and turn left. Three blocks later, we were on Main Street. We'd push open the big, wooden swinging doors and step inside. There it was... Field's Five and Dime in all of its glory! The familiar smell of oiled hardwood floors and cheap perfume greeted us. My friends couldn't decide which way to go first. After all, we had the whole, wide world stretched out before us! We scattered in all directions. As usual, I headed straight for the writing supplies. My sister, Ellen, made a beeline for the shelves of porcelain figurines. And my friends started browsing the book and toy displays.

The wooden floors squeaked the arrival of other customers. Soon the store was filled with Saturday shoppers. Even after I decided on my purchase, I still liked to look around. I'm not a shopper and a browser by nature, but there was just something about that store... just something about it. I never got tired of looking. It was a long time ago, but I still remember the dimestore days of my youth!

Looking forward to our Saturday ritual helped make saving money fun! Ellen and I would make frequent deposits in our piggybanks, and shake them often for a status report. Allowance, birthday money, shiny coins from a lost tooth... all went through the little piggy's slot. After all, we were kids on a mission. We had shopping to do!

The special day came! This was the day of the dumping. We knelt down on the hardwood floor beside our beds and started shaking. We'd shake and smile, shake and smile! The pennies, nickels, and dimes rolled out onto our bedspreads as the excitement filled the room. Then, the counting began! We zipped our fortunes into little change purses and tucked them safely inside our pockets. Off we went on the trip of a childhood!

We were careful shoppers. Taking an hour or more to decide on a ninety-cent purchase proved the point. But one dimestore day, Ellen and I learned a valuable lesson in caring. I had been in the writing supplies section of the store looking at tablets. I had carefully selected my favorites and was heading to the counter to pay for my purchase. A beautiful lace handkerchief in a glass display case caught my eye! My grandmother, Nina, always kept a nice, clean hanky tucked in the sleeve of her sweater. I knew that she would love that hanky! The price was twenty nine cents. I can *still* see that price tag in my mind. I started thinking. I would need to buy two. My grandmother, Nanny, kept her handkerchief in the chest pocket of her blouse. I knew that she would like the one with violet flowers on each corner.

I looked down at my writing tablets full of soft, clean paper— just waiting for my pencil to fill them with childhood thought and dreams. ***The rocking chair lessons Maw Great taught me came to mind! How was I going to spend the wisdom in that bank?*** I did some rather quick figuring to determine that I could get both handkerchiefs, rather than the tablets... and still have a few coins left. I could put my change back into my piggybank and start saving again for the tablets I wanted.

With a quick step in my walk, I returned to the writing supplies department and put my treasures back on the shelf. Feeling great inside, I paid for two beautiful handkerchiefs, and went to find my sister in the store. Ellen was in the housewares section holding two porcelain figurines, stamped "Made in Japan" on the bottom. She, too, had decided to buy gifts for our grandmothers, rather than spend the money on herself. She was determined to make both purchases, but was eleven pennies short. I could see the look of disappointment in her eyes. I smiled as I reached into my pocket for the needed change! **I'll never forget the feeling that gave me!** The memory of Ellen's smile is still a powerful reminder of the character that was built on that childhood decision.

Ellen and I left Field's Five and Dime that day with more than handkerchiefs and figurines. We carried with us the intrinsically wonderful feeling that came from *really* caring about our grandmothers and putting that love into action! Ellen and I were probably nine and eleven years old, but we learned some important wisdom that's stayed with us for life. I know that you can't buy wisdom in the Five and Dime, but that day my purchase was rich and rewarding enough to last me a long, long time!

Rocking Chair Wisdom: A lesson from your childhood isn't really learned until you put it to work in your life! You can bank on the rich deposits of rocking chair wisdom from the dimestore days of your youth. What will you buy with the pennies in your character bank?

43

THE
GENERATIONS CHANGE HANDS...

Lesson Sixteen

Be Yourself!

My great grandmother raised me on wisdom. Her rocking chair sayings were repeated so often during my childhood that I committed them to memory... and to my very character. Over the years they have defined me as a person, by guiding my thoughts and decisions.

> **Pretty is as pretty does.**
> **Do the right thing.**
> **Honesty is the best policy.**
> **Hard work never hurt anyone.**
> **You're judged by the company you keep.**
> **Just be yourself; don't try to be anyone else.**
> **Follow your heart.**

These are all sayings that I cut my wisdom teeth on as a child. I find myself using these same axioms with my own sons. We have traded places, Maw Great and I, for now I sit in the rocking chair of old— my own sons looking to me for advice and example. Singer, songwriter John Cougar Mellencamp's quote is appropriate here: "There is nothing more sad or glorious than generations changing hands." It *has* happened. And the glorious part is that the wisdom is changing hands, too.

Be yourself is the wisdom of the day. Like who you are; feel good about the you that you've chosen to be. As always, Æsop has a fable to enlighten us, *The Jay and the Peacock*. A Jay venturing into a yard where Peacocks used to walk, found there a number of feathers which had fallen from the Peacocks when they were moulting. He tied them to his tail and strutted down toward the Peacocks. When he came near them they soon discovered the cheat and, striding up to him, pecked at him and plucked away his borrowed plumes.

The Jay had no choice but to return to his own flock of Jays, who had watched him at a distance. They were equally annoyed with him, and told him so. Æsop's adage: *"It is not only fine feathers that make fine birds."* As Maw Great would say: *"Just be yourself."*

Being yourself is a fine thing. It takes confidence and courage...and commitment. In *The Winner Within,* Pat Riley shares his father's charge: "Every now and then, somewhere, some place, sometime, you are going to have to plant your feet, stand firm, and make a point about who you are and what you believe in. When that time comes...you simply have to do it." Like Lee Riley said, we have to know what it is that we believe in. Then the "standing up" becomes second nature. Freya Stark adds the finishing touches, "There can be no happiness if the things that we believe in are different from the things that we do."

When we know who we are, and we believe with a great faith that we are doing the right thing, we come to feel good about the person we've come to be. There is power, magic, excitement, and promise in it! That self esteem becomes a wonderful foundation for life. On it, we can build for the future.

Everyday in the classroom, I have my young students repeat the following rocking chair wisdom: *"Be in the right place at the right time, doing the right thing."* We say it when we're sharpening our pencils, we say it when we're lining up to go outside for recess, we say it when we're packing our bookbags at the end of the school day. On most days we squeeze in a dozen bits of wisdom without taking any time out of our schedules. And I know that by repeating it several times a day, 180 school days a year, that these five and six year old students internalize it. My hope is that it makes a positive difference in their lives, and that it will give them a moral rope to hang on to during the decision-times of their childhoods...and beyond. It's the least I can do because of the wisdom given me by my great grandmother. From the rocking chair in my own home, it's time to pass it on.

Rocking Chair Wisdom: Be yourself... listen to your internal wisdom... follow your heart... do the right thing! There's great power in it!

Lesson Seventeen

Letting Go... Helps You Go On!

My great grandmother was a hugger! As soon as we arrived at the screen door of her Kentucky farmhouse, the hugging began! When it was time to leave for home, the hugs started again. Hugs were her way of keeping us close. Maw Great could never get enough hugs from her five great grandchildren!

From my childhood, I learned the importance of pulling one another close. Time spent with someone you love is always the best part of your day. There is absolutely no substitute for it! It makes you feel good all over!

Maw Great taught me that: ***Coming together is a much-needed part of any relationship. But there will always come a time for letting go.*** Letting go is one of life's hardest-learned lessons. It's also the lesson that sometimes breaks the heart.

There were stories that I learned at Maw Great's knee about the times in life when we *need* to let go. Mrs. Pig had to let her sons go out into the world to seek their fortunes. The Three Little Pigs each had a choice about how to build for the future. Mrs. Pig had to learn the lesson of letting go. It's a natural part of life. It's also a lesson that I learned recently in a very personal way. My oldest son, Aaron, left home to make his own way in the world. He moved out of the nest... eight hundred miles away. It doesn't take much tuning-in to notice that my own heart is breaking. It's time for me to learn, again, the life-lesson of letting go. It's a lesson that Maw Great taught me those many years ago. But, no matter how prepared we are, it's still a hard lesson on the heart. Maw Great's death in 1967 was especially heart-breaking for me. Although a part of her has stayed with me over the years, it's like a part of me left with her. ***When you love someone, it's never easy to say goodbye.***

Rather than peruse the storybooks for a illustrative story on letting go, I'm going to share the powerful last-lesson that my mom ever taught me. It's a lesson on letting go that helped heal my broken heart. If you're dealing with a heartache of your own, it is my hope that Mom's lesson will help you heal, too.

One recent spring we learned that Mom's ship was on the final horizon—it was time for the definitive docking. The inevitability left me hopeless and heartbroken. The doctor's news was like the cold water of reality splashed on our faces: "One week." One week until the final docking.

The days passed. Our family pulled together. Mom taught us that. She taught us that with her life, and now— she was teaching us with her death. We cried together. We prayed together. And most importantly, we stayed together. The last days turned into weeks. We were grateful for the gift of each extra day.

We made the best of our time together. We talked... a lot. We got to know each other all over again. Some days we cried, together. There were the good days, though, the islands in the storm. We had fun— talking, teasing, laughing, and reminiscing. After all, we were family. And that's what families do best.

Mom hung on to life for that celebration of family. She hung on to life while we pulled each other close, making sure we would be able to weather the seas of life.... without her. We would, you know— she had taught us how. She became a maternal lightkeeper, protecting each of us as we sailed on... alone.

We kept watch, those weeks, docked at her side. **Death came quietly and peacefully in the night. There was nothing we could do to stop its coming.**

The doorbell shattered the silence of the night. It was time to take her lifeless body away. I followed the sidewalk out to the sleek, black hearse on the driveway. I used to rollerskate on this sidewalk, my mom watching from the window. Now, it was different. *The generations had changed hands.*

I stood, looking, for the longest time— begging minutes before the final goodbye. Then, I stood in the night quiet, watching as the hearse drove down the hill— until it was swallowed up by the darkness. For the very first time in my whole life... I felt truly alone.

The weeks of vigil inside the house were over. The family was now busy with the task at hand— removing the reminders of illness and suffering. I stood watching as the personal belongings of Mom were dismantled in the attempt. I joined the campaign in an effort to work through my own grief. Pulling off the bedsheets and covers, I thought back to all of the times we tried to keep Mom warm. Surely our love comforted her in recent weeks. It was then that I saw it— the lone blue sock... apart from the covers, alone on the floor. I picked it up and put it in my pocket... and went on with the work at hand.

When morning broke, I drove back home thinking— about the sock that had fallen from Mom's foot as they had taken her away in the night. I knew it had not been left by chance. I knew it was left... for me. Mom always had a way of getting through to me. It was no different, now. Even in death, she was teaching me lessons, planting seeds, and believing in me.

The lone blue sock is one of those seeds. It was the last thing my mom could leave for me. She left it so that I could heal. She knew that the lone blue sock would make me write, and she knew that by writing... I would finally be able to cry. I would finally be able to sail off on my own personal journey to acceptance and peace. I would finally be able to let the painful memories of her illness and death sink into the still and peaceful waters of life. I would then be able to adjust my sails towards the sun, remembering only... the good times.

It's been almost a year since I put that lone blue sock into my pocket. My mom took the other sock with her— as she sailed off into the night. And, because of her, I've learned to sail on... alone. The maternal lightkeeper taught me that.

These months later, I'm anxious to tell my story to my dad, brothers, and sisters. And, I'm anxious to hear their stories, too. Mom helped me deal with her passing by leaving me the lone blue sock. I'm sure that Mom left a little something special in each of our pockets that night. It was just like Mom to teach us one final lesson... the lesson of letting go.

Rocking Chair Wisdom: *Coming together is a wonderful thing! Cherish your time together. Remember, though, the lesson of the lone blue sock— the lesson of letting go.*

"Our self-confidence is built in direct proportion to the strength and structure of our character."

Lesson Eighteen

Take Time For Life's Simple Pleasures!

There are no two ways about it... I love the beach! Not the hotels, shops, restaurants, and entertainment on The Grand Strand... just the beach. There is nothing more wonderful than sitting in the sand on a cool morning and watching the sun rise out of the ocean in all of its splendor! And, when the pelicans fly by in formation, it's just the icing on the cake! I always watch the sun come up when I'm on the East Coast, and I always applaud afterward! It's such an incredible event; I always wonder why everyone else isn't out there, too.

When I travel to California each year, I plan my day around the sunset. When evening approaches, I head for the beach. It's a wonderful drive up the Pacific Coast Highway just as that big orange sun begins setting in the ocean! It truly takes my breath away! When I am at home in West Virginia, I have a West Coast friend who calls me from his car when he is making that drive from Santa Monica to Santa Barbara. He sends me the majestic Pacific Coast scenery from three thousand miles away! He holds the phone out the car window so I can *see* the sunset and *feel* the fresh ocean breezes! Ah-h! My mind just takes me away!

Another thing in life that makes me feel wonderful is watching the moon at night. From the time I could talk, I was asking to see the moon before going to sleep. Each night from the crib I would call out, "Wanna see the boon; wanna see the boon!" My grandmother would pick me up and take me to the window for a child-size glimpse of the moon that stilled me with wonder. These many years later, looking for the moon is still the last thing I do at night before going to bed. When I watch the moon and stars in the incredible night sky, I feel wonderful... and all is right with the world!

Whether it's a sunrise, sunset, walk on the beach, or glimpse of the night sky... there are things in life that make us feel great! They are usually the things in life that don't cost money, that come to us free for the taking. Maybe it's a drive on a sunny day, listening to a favorite CD on the stereo, a walk in the park, or time spent with someone you love. Whatever it might be, you know that you *always* feel better afterwards!

My great grandmother knew the meaning of true happiness. She lived every day appreciating life's simple pleasures. One of the fables Maw Great read to me often was Æsop's *The Mouse At The Seashore*. A young Mouse decided to go on a trip to the seashore. His parents urged him to reconsider, as the dangers were many. The Mouse was determined, because he had never seen the ocean. In the first light of dawn, he began his journey. Early on the way, a cat jumped out from behind a tree! The Mouse barely escaped with his life, leaving a part of his tail with the cat. By afternoon, the Mouse had been attacked by birds and dogs. He had lost his way several times. He was bruised and bloodied, tired and frightened.

At evening, the Mouse slowly climbed the last hill and saw the glorious seashore spreading out before him! He watched the waves rolling in and saw all of the incredible sunset colors fill the sky! As the little Mouse sat on top of the hill, the moon and stars began to dot the evening sky. He was overwhelmed by a feeling of deep peace and contentment. As Æsop points out: ***"All the miles of a hard road are worth a moment of true happiness."*** And, as Maw Great would say, ***"Take time for the simple pleasures of life."*** And with the start of a new day on the horizon, it's a good time for the reminder!

Rocking Chair Wisdom: *Life has many simple treasures to offer! Listen to your heart and discover the things that bring you real peace and contentment. Like the Mouse, we need to embark on our own journeys to happiness!*

Lesson Nineteen

Don't Do What's Easy...
Do What's Right!

It all started in the Delivery Room. I've *always* liked to write! I think I must have been born with a pencil in my hand. That's not the way my parents tell the story, but I just don't remember a time that I wasn't writing. If I have paper and a pencil, I'm a happy camper! My grandmother, Nanny, was always reading. Her bedroom was filled with wonderful books. She used to tell me that if you have a good book, you'll never be lonely. I believed her, but I always had my own personal version of happiness. And, it *always* involved writing. Writing in my journal, writing down my thoughts and feelings, writing letters to friends, writing down my goals and dreams... just writing! As long as that pencil was gliding across a sheet of paper, I was smiling! I know that I've written myself to this time and place in my life. Writing is just part of who I am. With that pencil of mine, I've etched out my character... and destiny.

Two friends of mine, Mike Mitchell and Bill Wotring, have just published a new book called *Speaking of Character.* One of the quotes in their book literally jumped off of the page at me! *"What is down in your well comes up in your bucket."* It's a great quote on character!

At my great grandmother's farm in Kentucky, there was a well in the backyard near the grape orchard. Sometimes Maw Great would let my sister and me fetch water for her. We'd take the big, heavy bucket and put it under the faucet— and start pumping! Ellen always had a fun spirit and a very strong arm. Before long we had the bucket overflowing, and we were drenched with water *and* giggles!

Our very characters are like a well. Here we store all of the traits we practice in our personal journeys of *becoming.* What goes down deep into the well are only the traits and qualities we *choose* to put there. Our attitudes determine our actions; our actions determine our character. It's as simple as that. And, if those traits aren't embedded deep down inside of us, they certainly cannot surface when we prime the pump!

My two sons, Aaron and Ben, have heard my own favorite piece of rocking chair wisdom over, and over... and over! I've told them that it's the *one* thing that I want them to remember from all the things that I've taught them: **"Even when it's tough, dig down deep inside yourself and find the strength to do the right thing. Don't do what's easy; do what's right!"** The advice is grand, but if the reserves are not down deep within our character, we certainly *won't* find them during the crisis and decision-times of our lives.

That's why it's so important to dig deeply. The small thoughts, deeds, and decisions of our lives all add up in big ways to determine our character. Each day, with the way we live and the choices we make, we are making deposits in that well. Honesty, integrity, loyalty, fairness, respect, responsibility, and caring are all desirable traits. But it takes *daily* commitment and practice to make those character traits a part of us. They are certainly powerful to tap into whenever the going gets tough! They can fill our buckets in wonderful ways!

Rocking Chair Wisdom: *Is your well deep and full of positive traits? Tap into the power! Fill it with all that is right and just. Then your life will be drenched with giggles... and goodness!*

Don't Look
In The Rearview Mirror Of Life!

Last year started off with a bang! Barely two weeks into the year, schools were closed for the Martin Luther King holiday. My friend, Linda, called and invited me to lunch. For an elementary school teacher, lunch usually means a thirty-minute period that consists of tying six shoes, putting on two band-aids, listening to a child tell the four-minute version about losing his first tooth, and returning at least one parent phone call. The way I figure it, that leaves about seventeen minutes for lunch. The thought of having a leisurely lunch in a restaurant was pure pleasure! So, off we went looking forward to our day! About ten steps away from the restaurant, a teenage girl with a car full of friends, came speeding around the corner, only to find that she couldn't make the turn. Something was in her way... and that something was *me!*

There was no time to think, no time to move. The car clipped me in the right knee. I fell toward her car. She kept on driving. I begged her to stop. She didn't. So, I pushed off from her car so my legs wouldn't be pulled under the spinning tires. She never did stop. She drove on to her day, taking mine right along with her. After a seven-hour hospital stay and six months of intense physical therapy, I did learn to walk on my right leg again. But during that time I wasted a lot of my life.

It was winter, and I was stuck home, alone. The dark, dreary days dragged on endlessly. I was in pain, and I was scared. I really thought my days of walking the beach and driving my little white sports car were over. I went from sixty to zero in 6.1 days! I didn't write during that time, I didn't read. I just lay in bed staring at the proverbial ceiling. For the first time in my life, I no longer felt like me. Gone were my enthusiasm and my passion!

The teachers at school sent me a little book of quotations. The one that I hung on to was this: ***"Adversity is never pleasant, but sometimes it's possible to learn lessons from it that can be learned in no other way."*** It sounded like rocking chair wisdom to me! It's just what I needed to hear! That little quote jump started my engine! I started working on my attitude so that I could find the hidden lesson from my accident. I quit thinking about the hit–and–run... and how that eighteen year old girl robbed me of a fun day and a healthy knee. Here I was, letting her rob me of my *life!* It's where I had to draw the line.

I knew I had to bring in the reserves to help fight this battle. I dug down deep into all of the rocking chair lessons I had been taught. I started looking through the picture albums of my life. I looked deeply into the faces of my family. I decided to tap into the power of their life lessons! It was time to put those lessons to work... for me. I reread old letters and stories; I watched old family movies; I thought about happier times. I used the powerful past to chart direction for the future! ***Instead of looking into the rearview mirror of misfortune, I decided to look ahead for the roadsigns of life that come with each new day.*** It was exciting... and even fun! And, just changing my attitude and perspective on my recouperation period changed everything! I'm now back to the old me... but better than ever. And, even my knee is healthier, too!

Rocking Chair Wisdom: *The rocking chair wisdom from your past stays with you for life! It's a powerful force in combating the negative influences that loom around adversity! Check under your hood, adjust your attitude... and you'll go from zero to sixty in no time at all!*

Lesson Twenty One

Be Accountable
For Your Words And Deeds!

My dad is always dishing out advice. He sits in his favorite chair near the fire-place saying, "I'll tell you one... thing..." and proceeds to give us a valuable lesson on life. One of the lessons I remember most is, ***"If you have a clear conscience, you can lie down and sleep anywhere. If you don't, not even a comfortable bed will help."*** I grew up very aware of the importance of having a clear conscience.

This past summer, when I was doing some research on character, I ran across the following illustration from an unknown author: ***Your conscience is a little triangle in your heart. It acts like a pinwheel. When you do good things, it does not rotate. When you do bad things, it turns around, and the corners hurt you a lot. If you keep on making bad decisions with your actions, the corners wear off; and when the little triangle spins around... it doesn't hurt anymore***. Wow! What a great analogy for teaching young children the workings of a good conscience! You can just see the power of that little triangle poking you back to the reality of your actions! You can also see the devastating results when the warnings are ignored.

My parents, grandparents, and Maw Great... all spent a lot of their time and energy teaching the five of us Austin children right from wrong. For that, I'll always be grateful! Each lesson was repeated over the years until we took it to heart. Then we each had a moral rope to hang on to during the decision times of childhood... and beyond. I'm glad that part of my heritage included that little triangle in my heart! My life certainly has been the better for it.

Growing up in a big family was wonderful! We had a happy and carefree childhood, and not a day goes by that I don't appreciate it and give thanks for my good fortune in life. But the heritage of morals and values I received has been the biggest blessing of all. **My family held me accountable for my words and deeds**. It's as simple as that. No excuses, no smoothing over wrongs, no looking the other way. If I made a mistake or did something wrong, I learned a lesson. My parents saw to it. No harsh criticism, no pejorative remarks, no scream-ing, no physical violence. They punished me, corrected me, and instructed me with lessons on the right paths to follow. If I made a good choice and acted on it, I reaped the benefits in wonderful ways! I felt good about myself, and therefore my self esteem and self respect soared! Each good decision laid a building block on the foundation of my character. During the formative years, a child's self concept is always under construction. **My self confidence was built in direct proportion to the strength and structure of my character.**

Today's world is so different. Morals, values, and respect seem to somewhat optional. It breaks my heart. And, it is certainly breaking up families and society. **At no time in history has any civilization tried to exist without a value system of right and wrong... like America is doing now.** I know that values are a necessary and needed part of good character... and a good life. I learned it right from the rocking chair of the past. My own sons have learned it, too. It's part of the heritage I have given them. Aaron and Ben are good kids, and I'm very proud of them! I guess at the ages of twenty-three and nineteen, they are not really kids anymore... but on their way to adulthood in a world that still needs discipline and direction. I'm usually proud of the choices they make in their day-to-day living. They make their share of mistakes, but they learn lessons that put them back on better paths. Because of rocking chair wisdom, their values are in place... for life! It is my parental hope that the choices they make throughout their lives will be rooted in that wisdom.

A favorite quote of mine, by Beverly Sills, reminds us... "There are no short-cuts to any place worth going." The same is true of character development. **Teach-ing values, respect, responsibility, and caring is everybody's job! Fami-lies must lead the way from the rocking chairs in their own homes.** Schools, churches, and society must help in the effort by reinforcing those lessons and holding all of us accountable. The wisdom gained from the rocking chair lessons of the past can *certainly* make the world a better place!

Rocking Chair Wisdom: A child's value system is in place by the age of twelve! Give your children instruction, bound-aries, and direction for their lives. Give them a moral rope to hang on to by teaching them right from wrong... and then holding them accountable. That little triangle in their hearts is the best gift you can ever give your children!

No One Said
Life Was Supposed To Be Fair!

No one ever said that life was supposed to be fair. At least that's what my great grandmother used to tell me. During my childhood, Maw Great read to me from a wonderful collection of books… nursery rhymes, fairy tales, fables, Bible stories, proverbs, and poetry. Together we rocked a thousand miles in that rocking chair of hers. And with each mile and each reading, I listened in on hundreds of stories about life. In none of those stories was life even close to being even-handed. **Life just isn't fair!** It's one piece of rocking chair wisdom that we all need to learn early in life. Then we can quit resisting the twists and turns on the road of life, and settle down and learn to enjoy the ride.

Most people only complain about the unfairness of life when they are faced with a problem or crisis. I suppose that's only natural. But, come to think of it, I usually don't hear too many complaints when life is unfair… to someone's *advantage!* As I see it, the Complaint Department of life has two windows. One window handles complaints about the negative unfairness of life, and the other window is for complaints about the positive unfairness of life. You can imagine the long line at the first window! I doubt if anyone has ever bothered to show up at the second window.

Personally, several things come quickly to mind when I think how unfair life has been to me. The day I was told that I had won a Milken Family Foundation National Educator Award was one of the most unfair things that ever happened to me! It was also one of my life's crowning moments. How could I possibly think that I was worthy of such a prestigious award when there are so many wonderful teachers out there in the world doing just what I do each and every day? And when I was handed the $25,000 check with the directive to make one of my *personal dreams* come true… well, it was just not fair. I didn't head for the Complaint Department. I savored the moment and thanked God for the blessing. And I'll spend each of my remaining days trying to live up to the honor. I suspect that any of us would do the very same thing.

Another example of life's unfairness is illustrated by my son, Ben. Three times in the last three years, he has been in a car wreck where the car was totaled. All three times, Ben should have been killed. The police told me that. The firemen at the scene told me that. The paramedics and the wrecker service workers reiterated the point. Ben has spent a lot of time thinking that life is unfair and that he is the most unlucky kid he knows. **Unlucky?!** A lot of talking on my part, plus lots of good old rocking chair wisdom has finally convinced Ben that he is the *luckiest* kid of all! He has walked away from each accident without a scratch! His Guardian Angel sure has been working overtime! **It's not fair, but this mom is surely grateful!** Ben has a new quote that I gave him and his friends to hang on to: "Never drive faster than your guardian angel can fly!" I know in my heart that Ben, too, is glad that life *isn't* fair!

As you'll see in this next story, life can be painfully unfair at times. My son, Aaron, was at work one hot, summer day at a restaurant in a neighboring town. He saw a homeless dog walking the streets. Dirty, diseased, disfigured, and dehydrated... the little dog was literally starving to death. Aaron is a compassionate kid. He took bowls of water and food outside for the little fellow. Seeing that the dog was seriously ill, Aaron took the necessary action to make sure that the dog received medical help. Aaron didn't even tell me about it for a very long time. He needed time to heal. It bothered Aaron to think that this little dog had suffered for many days. He felt that life had dealt this animal an unfair hand. Some people in the neighborhood *must* have seen that dog walking around hungry and sick. And, as unfair as it was, no one took action. A treasured quote by Mark Twain comes to mind: *"Thunder is good, thunder is impressive; but it is lightning that does the work."* Some people talk as loudly as thunder about being good and fair people. But, they do little in life to back up their words. **Thank God that Aaron is a lightning-kind-of-kid!** That little dog taught Aaron a lesson about life that will stay in his heart for a very long time.

The journey through life is an unfair one. For that, we should all be grateful. If we were always treated as we deserved to be treated, it could be a very different world. But we are often treated to special surprises, good fortune, unexpected goodness, lucky breaks, and second chances. I'm fairly certain that we all expect the good and bad in life, but I'm not sure that we chalk up the undeserved goodness to the *unfairness of life*. Perhaps it's a new perspective for you to reflect upon. So, sit down in the rocking chair and think about it for a bit. And, while you're there, count your blessings... by name. Today, I'm counting Aaron and Ben.

Rocking Chair Wisdom: Life isn't fair. So, quit complaining about the twists and turns on the road of life. Sit down in the rocking chair and enjoy the ride! There's a hidden lesson in each mile!

Lesson Twenty Three

Laughter Is The Best Medicine!

The score is in! It's 15 to 400! Adults do it fifteen times each day. And, kids really out-do us! Each day, kids laugh over four hundred times! It's incredible, isn't it? With only sixteen waking hours in the day, that means that kids are laughing and smiling, pretty much nonstop. I guess that's the true essence of childhood. No pressures, no worries... just pure enjoyment. And that's the way it should be. Now you understand why I enjoy teaching young children so much! Their attitudes and laughter are contagious. Kids are an inspiration to us all!

When I was growing up, we sure did our share of laughing. Gee, did we ever have fun! With three adults and five children in the Austin household, something funny was always going on! And, I'll have to say... we really enjoyed each other! Cultivating a sense of humor was an important part of our upbringing. Dad was always telling jokes. In fact, he's still telling the same ones from twenty-five years ago! We still laugh because we all get a kick out of how much fun he has telling them.

On the farm in Kentucky, my great grandmother had a favorite saying to support our giggles, *"Laughter is the best medicine."* The editors of *Readers' Digest* think so, too. The magazine devotes several pages each month to that very topic. Scientific research shows that laughter is healthy. It's a wonderful release for stress and tension. It lowers blood pressure and increases blood circulation. And, it produces endorphins in our bodies that are used to fight off bad cells, disease, and infection. We are learning that when faced with the deadlines, dilemmas, and difficulties of life... that humor is *just what the doctor ordered!*

The way I see it from the rocking chair of the past, **laughter is the sign of a happy home.** It warms the heart, brings families together, and mends broken hearts. Some of my best childhood memories are full of laughter! Looking back, we were always teasing and joking with each other. It's a wonderful legacy for all of us Austin kids!

When my dad was at work, we kids took advantage of mom. Looking back, I wonder how she survived with the odds of five-to-one. But she loved to hear us laugh and was a good sport to put up with all of our giggles and pranks. We'd even get Nanny giggling and in on the act. Gee, how I miss those days on College Hill with my brothers and sisters! Before anyone gets the chance to tease me and tell you, I'll go ahead and admit it... I'm the oldest kid in the Austin family. Ellen, Stephanie, Tom, and Pat never let me forget it, either. They always introduce me as their *oldest sister, Deb*. It's definitely a thrilling event! Now, that they've done it for so long, I'll have to admit that I'd be disappointed if they stopped. It's one of those things we've laughed about for so long, I know I'd really miss it.

Some people have a wonderful laugh! Just hearing them belt it out makes everyone feel good all over. My grandmother, Nina, had one of those laughs. When my brother, Tom, was younger, he was always saying and doing the cutest things. There was never a more clever kid than Tom! Nina would get so tickled over his antics, that she'd giggle and giggle. Pretty soon the laughter was contagious, and we were all laughing uncontrollably. Those were the good old days! My sister, Stephanie, was a "little" on the clumsy side growing up. She gave us lots of endorphins during those years. She could hardly walk across the floor without falling and causing a commotion. She grew out of it to become one of the most graceful athletes ever on a basketball court. She went in for layups with the ease and grace of a ballerina! Wow! It was incredible! That talent took her all the way to college... on a scholarship.

Ellen is funny by nature. She inherited Dad's warm and wonderful quick-wit. She's the one who can dish it out, right back to him. I just love being around her! I enjoy her... and the laughter. Pat is the youngest in the Austin family. He's the most quiet, but when he comes out with something, it's worth waiting for! Pat and Tom live out of state, so we're all together only twice a year. It's definitely not often enough, but when the big weekend comes and all of us are together... well, it's a laugh-a-minute!

We Austins have our reputation. We love life, and love to have a good time. We're famous for it! Sometimes, we feel and act like kids... laughing and smiling hundreds of times a day. But, when you think about it, there are worse things to be remembered for.

On June 13th of last year, I got some really tough news. I knew that it was going to take a lot of personal discipline and effort, in the fight to keep my head above water. I spent one afternoon looking through the thousands of pictures I have from over the years. I pulled out my favorites... 62 of them... from the happiest times of my life. I took the door in my study and framed the pictures to cover the entire door. I call it my own personal, bigger-than-life... *en-__door__-phin*! I spend a few minutes each day looking back at happier times and drawing strength from them. I remember the fun, the laughter, and the love in all of those pictures! That *door* has done wonders for me! And, it has helped pull me through a really tough time. Maw Great was right! **Laughter is the best medicine!** My *life* is living proof!

Rocking Chair Wisdom: Laughter is the best medicine! It is also a healthy way to keep your life in balance. Be aware of the number of times each day that you laugh and smile. Leave the teens behind, and start now... working your way to the hundreds!

"Teaching values, respect, responsibility, and caring is everybody's job! Families must lead the way from the rocking chairs in their own homes."

Lesson Twenty Four

All Work And No Play...
Makes Jack A Dull Boy!

I can't help it... I like having fun! I even like the sound of the word. And whenever I write the word, I always put an excitement mark after it! Life is much too short not to include it in your day. Now, don't get me wrong. I'm not irresponsible. I'm about the most responsible person I know. And believe me, it's been a difficult task for me to keep up the balance. I'm serious about life! I believe in working hard, being productive, doing the right thing, making a difference, learning new things, contributing to our world, and... having fun! Even if I work hard to make this world a better place, who would want to be around me if I didn't have even a spark of fun? That's where the excitement comes in!

I get excited about things! Meeting new people, getting new ideas, celebrating a child's *Lightbulb Day,* getting a love note in the mail, driving with the t-tops out in my sports car, listening to really great music, watching the pelicans fly in formation, talking a walk on a fall day, writing late at night, watching old clips of Larry Bird playing basketball, seeing the full moon come up out of the ocean... the list goes on! My motto is: ***"Be on fire for something! Live passionately, enthusiastically, and fully!"*** That very thought is one of many taped to the inside of my bathroom mirror. It helps me get each day off to a positively great start!

During the week, I work hard! I put in a full day at Lakewood School in the classroom with those wonderful *K Kids!* The quote that I have on my classroom door says it all. It's from The Washington Post editor, Katharine Graham: **"To love what you do and feel that it matters, how could anything be more fun!"** Kindergarten is a great place to spend your day if you want to have fun! Kids are experts at it! They can really teach us a thing or two about enjoying life. We adults need to tune-in and learn from them. Each weekday evening, I work towards my goals... writing articles, columns, and books; planning my seminars and trainings; corresponding with exciting people from across the country; and reading and researching to learn new things. That all sounds like a lot of work (and it is!), but I love it so much that it transcends the *have-to-do-it list* to the *just-gotta-do-it* category of fun!

But, oh, when the weekend comes! Now, it's time to get really busy... having fun! Dinner with friends on Friday night is a great way to balance out the responsible work-week. I need that fun to help me from crashing and burning under the responsibilities of being a single parent and a dedicated teacher. It's my weekend assignment to enjoy a little of life. And I never feel guilty about taking a little time for me! It keeps me passionate and enthusiastic about life! And, when I'm really feeling the pressure, I take off for a few days at the beach. Just looking out at the vastness of the ocean really helps to put the problems of life into perspective. And basking in all of that sunshine and fresh ocean air doesn't hurt, either!

The key is getting to know yourself... what you *want* and what you *need*... and the difference between the two. I must say that the journey is an exciting one! My great grandmother taught me that. She knew well that we all needed a balance of work and play in our lives. Maw Great used to say, ***"All work and no play... makes Jack a dull boy!"***

Maw Great taught me to look for signs that we have put fun on the backburners of life. She had this special teapot on her woodburning stove. She loved to tell the story of that teapot. She said that ***even when the teapot was up to its neck in hot water, that it still kept on whistling!*** It's a great piece of rocking chair wisdom! It's one of my Dad's favorite memories of Maw Great! Her teapot spent its life in hot water, yet never lost its enthusiasm for the job. **It literally whistled its way from life on the hot seat... to a whistling good time!**

Have you put fun on the back burners of your life? Get in touch with the child in you! Of course, you don't have to wait until the weekend to have fun! Start adding a little fun to each and every day. Everyone will enjoy their time with you, and you may even like yourself a little better, too!

Rocking Chair Wisdom: Put fun back on the front burners of your life! Be on fire for something! Live passionately, enthusiastically, and fully... with steady doses of fun in your life!

References

BOOKS

Æsop. *Æsop's Fables.* Various collections.

Mitchell, Dr. William. 1995. *Winning in the Land of Giants.* Nashville: Thomas Nelson Publishers.

Mitchell, Dr. William. 1986. *The Power of Positive Students.* New York: Bantam Books.

Mitchell, Dr. William. 1990. *Power of Positive Students Workshop.* Myrtle Beach, South Carolina: Billy Mitchell, Inc.

Riley, Pat. 1993. *The Winner Within.* New York: The Berkley Publishing Group.

Ziglar, Zig. 1987. *Top Performance.* New York: The Berkley Publishing Group.

Williams, Margery. 1936. *The Velveteen Rabbit.* New York: Doubleday and Company.

Mitchell, Michael and **Dr. William Wotring.** 1996. *Speaking of Character.* Myrtle Beach, South Carolina: POPS International, Inc.

Brown, Les. 1992. *Live Your Dreams.* New York: Avon Books.

Fulghum, Robert. 1988. *All I Really Need to Know I Learned in Kindergarten.* New York: Villard Books.

Covey, Stephen R. 1989. *The Seven Habits of Highly Effective People.* New York: Simon and Schuester.

Hill, Napoleon. 1937. *Think and Grow Rich.* New York: Random House.

Hill, Napoleon and **W. Clement Stone.** 1960. *Success Through a Positive Mental Attitude.* New York: Prentice Hall, Inc.

Cypert, Samuel. 1991. *Believe and Achieve: W. Clement Stone's 17 Principles of Success.* New York: Avon Books.

Piper, Watty. 1930. *The Little Engine That Could.* New York: Putnam Publishing Group.

Robbins, Tony. 1994. *Giant Steps.* New York: Simon and Schuster.

FABLES FROM ÆSOP

The Crab and His Mother
The Hare and the Tortoise
The Donkey, the Cock, and the Lion
The Mountain in Eruption
The Crow and the Pitcher
The Jay and the Peacock
The Bulls and the Lion

The Bundle of Sticks
The Shepherd's Boy and the Wolf
The Olive Tree and the Fig Tree
Hercules and the Wagoner
The Farmer and His Sons
The Mouse at the Seashore

FAIRY TALES

From England

The Three Little Pigs (collected by Joseph Jacobs)
Jack and the Beanstalk (collected by Joseph Jacobs)
The Cock, the Mouse, and the Little Red Hen (Felicite Le Fevre)

From France

Cinderella (collected by Charles Perrault)
Sleeping Beauty (collected by Charles Perrault)
Pinocchio (collected by Carlo Lorenzini)

From Germany

The Frog Prince (collected by William and Jacob Grimm)
Rapunzel (collected by William and Jacob Grimm)
Cat and Mouse in Partnership (collected by William and Jacob Grimm)

PERSONAL CONVERSATIONS

Austin, Margaret McKibben
Austin, T.H. Jack
Brown, Ben
Brown, Aaron
Goff, Betty
McKibben, Eugenia Grobmeier
Mitchell, Dr. William
Rubenacker, Margarette French McKibben

About The Author

DEB AUSTIN BROWN

Deb is a teacher by heart. She has been honored with several teaching awards, including the Milken Family Foundation National Educator Award and The Ashland Oil Teacher Achievement Award. Her work transcends the classroom to include giving presentations, keynotes, and seminars for parents and educators across America.

She spends her free time writing, beachcombing, and watching the incredible night sky! Deb lives in her hometown of St. Albans, West Virginia with her two sons, Aaron and Ben. She spends her summers in Garden City Beach, South Carolina.

More Lessons
From The Rocking Chair!

People from across the country have been writing to tell us that this collection of *Lessons From The Rocking Chair* has touched their lives. They are remembering the wonderful heritage of stories from their own families! Perhaps reading this book has helped to bring back a special memory of a lesson you learned growing up. From the front porch swing, from the edge of a featherbed, from the kitchen table, and from the rocking chair... stories have bonded us to our loved ones, enriched our lives, taught us right from wrong, and helped shaped our very characters.

Perhaps you would be interested in telling a story from your past and sharing the wisdom of its lesson. Please send us your *lesson from the rocking chair* for consideration in our next published collection. Mail all stories to:

CHARACTER
DEVELOPMENT
GROUP

P.O. Box 9211
Chapel Hill, NC 27515-9211
Attn: Deb Brown

For ordering additional copies of this work, or more
information about Character Development Group's other resources for character
education...

Call (919) 967-2110
Fax (919) 967-2139
E-mail respect96@aol.com
www.CharacterEducation.com